MEMORY

Frustrated by your Forgetfulness?

"…humbly accept <u>the word planted in you,</u> which can save you" James 1:21 (NIV)

"Get wisdom, get understanding; <u>do not forget my words</u> or swerve from them." Proverbs 4:5 (NIV)

Memorizing the four gospels of the New Testament is just the beginning.

Have you ever dreamed about having a photographic memory? Imagine the unlimited possibilities if only you could retain everything you read. Inside you will find fun, exciting and effective ways to build your memory power. Dramatically improving your religious studies, success at work, school, and in your social life.

Unleash the Genius Within You!

"In an intellectual view, the endless opportunities offered in this book, opens the doors to higher education and knowledge. The possibilities seem to be presented as Infinity!"

—Alan Echols—Author

"The title: The Gift of Knowledge-truly explains it all. This book has helped me with my memory and benefited my Bible study."

—Kenneth Hoffman

"I was persuaded that I was predestined to a lifetime of forgetfulness. Now I feel blessed with the incredible gift of memory and knowledge."

—Jason Lee Norman

MEMORY

◆

The Gift of Knowledge

How-To Memorize the Four Gospels of the New Testament in One Week

Timothy L. Twitty

iUniverse, Inc.
New York Lincoln Shanghai

MEMORY
The Gift of Knowledge

iUniverse books may be ordered through booksellers or by contacting:

iUniverse
2021 Pine Lake Road, Suite 100
Lincoln, NE 68512
www.iuniverse.com
1-800-Authors (1-800-288-4677)

ISBN-13: 978-0-595-37506-6 (pbk)
ISBN-13: 978-0-595-81899-0 (ebk)
ISBN-10: 0-595-37506-5 (pbk)
ISBN-10: 0-595-81899-4 (ebk)

Printed in the United States of America

Contents

DEDICATION

To my late grandmother, Leoda Halford, who taught me that no matter how hard life seems to be, changes comes from within. She was my mother, grandmother and best friend.

To my eldest brother, Johnny Twitty, who I never had the opportunity to get to know. He is loved and cherished through my heart and spirit.

To Frank and Diane Adams, who truly brought me to know Christ by adopting me as a son and showing me how Christian love can change even the hardest of hearts.

To Melvin Claussen and in memory of Ethel Claussen, who was as close to family as life would permit. I thank you for helping to raise me, and showing me affection during the hard years of being a teen.

To all who seek better memory, and decided to use it to advance yourself in the Word of God. There is no higher knowledge or wisdom without Christ.

To the Lord Jesus, in whose name all our petitions are made, heard and answered.

ACKNOWLEDGMENT

To my most wonderful grandparents, I like to thank you grandpa Merle Halford for raising me as your own son, and for being a model worth looking up to. And my grandma Julie Adee, who through her many years, and impressive accomplishments, she still has a special beauty within. I thank you both for your love and emotional support.

I want to thank two sets of parents. First my mother and her wonderful husband. George and Mary Perry, for being everything that a son could ask for. Thank you for being exactly who you are. Second, my mother and father in law. Judy and Stan Hall, who accepted me with open arms, loved me as a son, and treated me as a friend. I thank you for your work and support in helping me get my work into print.

I need to give special attention to my sister Kathy Harmon and my brother's Steve Twitty and Shea Coker. If anyone showed me the ropes to life, it was through the blood of family that got me this far.

Sara Harrah, my wonderful niece who loved me, pushed me, and encouraged me while working on my many projects, her many letters brought me to the reality of this world.

To the rest of my family: Ted Hall, Tiffany and Casey Wallace, and my uncles George, Pat, Dick, Ron, and Tom Adee. I pray that God will bless you and you will find comfort in His Spirit.

To my wife who stood by my side through all the rough times. Allowing me to burden her with all my crazy idea's. Thank you for your love, friendship, and support.

And lastly I want to acknowledge my many wonderful friends: Jennifer Bute, Betty Forbes, Julie Sibbit, Carri Harkness, Mike Mitchel, Maryja Harris, Scott Shampine, and Teresa "Tessi" Lyons.

CHAPTER ONE
HOW MEMORY WORKS

How Memory Works

Your mind is made up of many storage bins. Each bin is like a file cabinet. We see something, hear or smell something and our mind automatically pick the sight, sound or smell and places it into one of our bins or file cabinets. Each bin or file is separate. One file is for just what we see. The other is a file for what we hear and the last one is for what we smell.

Everything we see, smell or hear is filed away in our brains. Much of the information goes untouched for a long period of time. Other memories are used more often.

Have you ever wondered why we can not remember everything? Here is an example: Your in your early teens, you "date" many different peers. None of them stand out any more special then the next. Twenty years later someone asks you if you can name every person you were friends with from age 10 to age 20. You might name many of them as you think back. The next day a person walks past you and the way this particular stranger smells brings back instantly a vivid memory of someone in your distant past. Than you realize that the day before, when you was trying to recall old names, you did not even remember this person at all. How does this happen? Every memory is tossed in a file cabinet with thousands of other lost memory files. Stored away as quick thoughts. But then there is "the important" files we do not want to lose so we place them in the top draw with all the "do not forget" files. We neatly place these thoughts in a file folder and place a tag on it that will help us find the information quickly when needed. These files might include:

> Your new bosses name
> Your wedding anniversary
> What day and time your favorite T.V. show airs
> What day the trash man comes
> School work your soon to take a test on

So if we mentally tag only our important files, why did that smell take us back 20 years? In our memory files we might tag the file of our favorite T.V. show as: "Leave it to Beaver". So when we look for that file we think of "Leave it to Beaver", and the file is pulled out of the top drawer and opened up. Instantly we recall the last episode, who Beavers family is, his friends, what he wears, how he talks and etc.

But for those memories that we do not take the time to tag. Our minds automatically slaps a small unnoticeable tag on it without us noticing. This tag is not as purposeful as our "titled" tags:

Bosses name
Wedding date
Leave it to Beaver
Trash pick-up on Tuesday
Test in history-presidents

The tag that our mind places on memory might be a particular sound like a bird, or a way a can of soda sounds when being opened. Think of how your pet comes running each time you open a can or bag. Even animals are accustomed to associating a sound to memories. The pet might think: "What does the can being open remind me of? Oh yea, that great tasting meal I had last night." Our mind might tag our memory with sight or smell. In the case of the stranger who walked by you, causing you to travel back 20 years. The tag might be a feeling. An example might be how the temperature and sunlight on your skin reminds you of the vacation you took to the beach a few years back.

Now you might be wondering how all this information is going to help you now. How will this help me increase my memory? The answer lies in understanding memory. Recognizing that to increase our memory, we must learn to take the time to tag more memory instead of just dumping it in with thousands of other unorganized memories.

The more memory we put in a file folder, tagged and placed in our top drawer, the greater our memory, knowledge and intelligence will grow.

Let's say your anniversary is coming up and you absolutely do not want to forget it again this year. So what do you do? First you might write it on the calendar. Then you might place a note on the car dash. You program your computer to say "anniversary" every time you turn it on or check your E-mail. Why do we do this? Why do we place repeated reminders everywhere? Because we want to place a reminder in more than one place and deliver to us in more than one form. Sight and sound.

The same goes with memory. If we want to memorize something we might first tag and file it in the top drawer of our reading memory. An example is how our new boss spells his name. But for better, longer lasting memory, we might make a back-up file and tag it with a visual tag. What the boss looks like. This file goes to a file cabinet located in a different room in our brain. Next we might create a "smell" tag. Maybe the boss wears a unique cologne or perfume. Maybe a mix of smoke and garlic. The scent or smell file is once again a complete separate file.

The more places you store information in your mind. The more likely it is that the information will persist and can be found at a later date. Remember that these tabs or files can be visual, auditory, smells, or many other unique forms.

Look at the word "beach". You can not help yourself from opening the file that tells you that B-E-A-C-H spells beach. Which means a sandy area surrounding water. The next file that is opened is the visual file. Weather you have been to a beach or seen it on T.V., you can "see" sand, waves, and seagulls in your mind. And if your one of the lucky ones who visited an oceanfront beach, you might even open the "taste" file and recall the salty taste of the sea water. Next you may open the "audio" file. Where you can "hear" the waves crashing against the shore, and the seagulls crying.

To manipulate the benefits of creating multiple files, you may have to devote some effort to finding different tags and connections that are easiest for you to recall. At least when you first begin. Using the techniques in this book will help you find connections, files and tags instantly. And will help bridge gaps between lost memories.

Some people prefer to use their visual files by creating a picture of whatever it is they are trying to learn. This way is one of the easiest and most effective way to remember. Others have a great memory for taste and smells. They remember grandma by the smell of grandmas' baking, not so much of what grandma looks like. Other people remember sounds better, and for these people, it might be easier to tag files with sound: The word Autonomous would be remembered as rhyming with: A ton of mess. Meaning: Uncontrolled. These people might think that a ton of mess comes from being uncontrolled like a child without rules.

Whatever your particular associations. You can create a better memory pattern by learning to place new information in as many file cabinets as you possibly can. As you confront new information and ideas you want to remember, consider them from as many angles or files as you can possibly think of.

Imagine your on that beach we pulled out of your memory file and you find a really awesome shell. You pick it up and examine it by turning it in your hands. What you are doing is creating a visual file of that shell. As you hold that shell in your hand, what is the first thing you want to do? That's right. You want to put it to your ear and see if it really sounds like the ocean. Therefore, creating a new "audio" file. You will notice that each perspective of examining that shell creates new files and therefore, new places for storage.

Filing or tagging in visual images (creating pictures in your mind) is particularly useful for most of us because vision is one of the strongest memory systems. About 40 percent of the brain is devoted to vision functions-more than any other function. That is why your assimilation of recalling pictures and faces are better than your ability of recalling words or concepts.

As you continue in this book, you will be taught many mnemonic techniques which are sometimes dismissed as mental shortcuts. Some believe that these shortcuts create only game-show memory. But learning how to use them is a good exercise in memory storage involving interactive imagery. Which means creating pictures or stories to help you place, store, tag and recall things you want to learn or memorize. Regardless of how much or how long. Storage in your file cabinets is key to a great memory, and the best way to use the files is the ability to use imagery.

CHAPTER TWO
FOOD AND MEMORY

Dietary Guidelines for Americans

Free Radicals

Eating for Antioxidents

Food and Memory

Most of us know that nutrition effects our health. Yet we seem to have a difficult time comparing what we eat to how well our bodies perform. If we learn how food effects our body and what food will create energy and function and in what amount we need these foods. We can increase performance, memory, and control a lot of our emotional issues.

What is the association between what you eat and drink and how well you can recall? Let's look first at why what we eat and the nutrition that we consume has a significant impact to our memory's functioning.

Improper nutrition can lead to neurological and other health problems. Also insufficient nutrition may make us more exposed to other diseases. Nutrition is an important consideration when it comes to memory because it can affect our over-all health.

A healthy memory requires a healthy diet. Nutrition directly effects memory fitness. What we eat and drink gives us the energy that our brains need to recall. Unhealthy eating patterns can make it difficult to keep your memory in order. We need to understand that our eating habits can specifically affect memory due to diseases such as hypertension and diabetes. These diseases are coherently caused by how or what we eat. There are many different factors in health and diseases that causes unhealthy bodies which in turn causes unhealthy memory ability.

One of the best things you can do for your memory health is simply eat a healthy diet. Brain cells need sufficient nutrition for normal activity. Current dietary guidelines suggest that a varied diet that is low in fat and high in fruits, whole grains, vegetables, and protein is best. Fruit and vegetables can also be an significant food source of antioxidants, food components that may provide protection from disease and aging.

Dietary guidelines for Americans

Governmental recommendations to prevent disease and over nutrition, first published by the U.S. Department of Agriculture and the U.S. Department of Health and Human Services in 1980 and updated in 1995 (Fourth edition). The following seven recommendations for all healthy Americans two years of age and older, are quoted as follow:

1. Enjoy eating a variety of foods

2. Balance the food you eat with physical activity-maintain or improve your weight.
3. Choose a diet with plenty of grain products, vegetables and fruit.
4. Choose a diet lean in fat, saturated fat, and cholesterol.
5. Choose a diet moderate in sugar.
6. Choose a diet moderate in salt and sodium.

You can profit more fully from your diet if you spread your nutritional intake evenly over the course of the day. Trying to get all your nutrients at one meal will not work. It is best to eat various meals throughout the day. Your body will absorb nutrients more efficiently, permitting you to get the most from your diet.

It is important to not forget the liquids in our diets. Receiving enough liquids to keep our body hydrated is significant to all of our body tissues, including our brains. Most of us do not drink enough water. On the other hand we fool ourselves in believing that all the coffee, soda and tea we drink is fulfilling the need our body have for liquids. Caffeine actually causes the body to lose fluid. Low fluids in our bodies may result in memory loss and confused thinking.

Your daily food intake should meet your major nutritional needs. However, there may be times when you do not eat as well as you should, or your diet may not routinely include sources for certain essential vitamins or minerals. The best way to be sure your body is receiving all of it's required nutritional needs of essential vitamins and minerals is to take a multivitamin which is a magnificent nutritional back up. Be sure to use it with a good diet, and not as a replacement for a healthy diet. Getting into the habit of taking a multivitamin can guarantee you will get sufficient amounts of substances you might otherwise miss.

One of the most dominant theories of aging and memory loss is the free radical theory.

Free Radicals

Free radicals are damaging molecules or ions that often contain oxygen. Many health conditions are linked to free radicals damage, such as, cancer, high blood pressure, Alzheimer's disease, senility, and many more diseases.

According to the free radical theory, free radicals causes damage that results in disease and aging. Antioxidants are substances that absorb free radicals, thereby protecting us from the harm they do.

Antioxidants are significant in protecting memory function. Researchers found that higher levels of antioxidants in the blood were associated with better memory. Other researchers found that vitamin E, considered by many to be one of the most effective antioxidants, slowed the progression of Alzheimer's disease.

It is a good idea to add an antioxidant to your diet. While your multivitamin probably includes various antioxidants, you can supplement your diet further by adding an additional dose of vitamin C, vitamin E, or B-1 to your vitamin intake.

Vitamin C:

Vitamin C has a little known but essential function in the central nervous system, including the brain and spinal cord. The central nervous system is the most significant part of the body.

There is no organ or area of the body that contains more unsaturated fats than the central nervous system. This makes it a prime target for attack by free radicals. Vitamin C is one of the most effective antioxidants and free radical fighters.

Vitamin E:

Vitamin E is the major antioxidant in the body, the property for which it is best known. It stops free radicals, highly reactive molecules that can attack neighboring molecules and damage polyunsaturated fatty acids in membrane lipids, proteins and DNA, damaging cells and leading to disease. Free radical damage is linked to cancer, heart disease, cataracts and aging. This vitamin plays an significant role in the immune system, the nervous system and the endocine (hormonal) system. ***Vitamin E should not be taken together with iron because they interfere with each other.

Vitamin B-1:

Vitamin B-1 is also known as thiamin. Thiamin deficiency can masquerade itself as senility. Lack of memory or exhibits of mental confusion is found in Alcoholics who lack thiamin. The need of thiamin supplementation is not needed for memory if thiamin deficiency is not involved. Deficiency of B-1 is not uncommon. Symptoms of moderate deficiency include fatigue, apathy, nausea, irritability, depression, and loss of appetite. Consuming large amounts of sugar found in candy and sodas' increases the need for thiamin.

Eating for Antioxidants

You do not need to take extra vitamins to get your daily dose of antioxidants. Listed below are some foods that are high in antioxidants:

Beets	Blueberries
Plums	Potatoes
Broccoli	Red Grapes
Corn	Red Peppers
Kale	Spinach
Kiwi	Strawberry
Oranges	Pink Grapefruit
Nuts	White Grapefruit
Eggs	Leafy Vegetables

CHAPTER THREE
MEMORY SUPPLEMENTS

Supplements Explained

Memory Supplements

We often wonder what supplements we should take to help our memory. It is important to remember that the pills that we take can not by themselves help you have a photographic memory. This type of thinking would be like believing that you can eat fatty foods, never exercise and to keep from having a heart attack, all you need to do is take a aspirin. Or you eat cakes, chips, fatty foods and drink sodas all day and believe that taking a diet pill without exercise will make you loss weight.

Memory is contingent on many factors. The most important factor is that we eat a well-balanced diet, drink lots of water and take a multivitamin. The second factor is exercise. Exercise means both physical and mental. The brain is a muscle that is dependent on blood and oxygen, and mental exercises like doing cross-word puzzles, or practicing memorizing, reading books or learning memory techniques. Working the brain muscle is a lot like working the body muscles. If you don't use them, they break down. If you work them, they become bigger and stronger.

When you eat a good healthy diet, drink water, and exercise. You may want to add a few supplements to help you improve your memory even more.

Listed below is the supplements that I would recommend. But if you are on medication, or have high blood pressure, I would talk to your doctor before taking any of these supplements. Because even though most of them are found in your everyday diet, increasing the amounts could have an adverse side effect to what prescriptions you may be on.

1. Mitochondrial Protectors:
    CoQ1 0
    Acetyl-L-carnitine
    Alpha Lipoic Acid

2. Antioxidant Supplements:
    Vitamin C
    Vitamin E
    Vitamin B-1

3. B Complex Vitamins
    B-1 (Thiamin)
    B-2 (Riboflavin)

B-3 (Niacin)
B-5 (Pantothenic Acid)
B-6 (Coenzyme A)
B-12 (Pyridoxal Phosphate)
Folic Acid
Biotin

4. Herbs
Gingko Biloba

5. Smart Oils (Omega 3 & 6)
Flexseed Oil
Fish Oil

6. Phosphatidylserine (PS)

7. Lecithin

8. DHEA

9. DMAE

Supplements Explained

What we eat can have a powerful impact on how clearly we think and remember. Knowing a little about each supplement will help you decide which supplement will be best for your use.

Mitochondrial Protectors:

Mitochondria are energy factories of the cell where both energy and energy by-products (free radical pro-oxidants) are produced.

Coenzyme Q10 (CoQ10):

Recommended Dosage: 30-300 mg once daily with food and preferably with vitamin E.

Description: Fat-soluble antioxidant stabilizes the mitochondrial membrane, helps mitochondrial energy production, and has antioxidant properties.

Acetyl-L-carnitine:

Recommended Dosage: 100 mg to 2 grams, in the morning.

Description: Another noteworthy brain enhancer, acetyl-L-carnitine, heightens our natural capacity to transport fat across cell membranes so that the energy furnaces in each cell, or mitochondria, have more fuel to burn. Acetyl-L-carnitine carries out the same functions as plain carnitine, the body's own substance, but does them better. It energizes the brain, slows its aging and protects brain cells. It acts as a brain antioxidant.

Alpha Lipoic Acid:

Recommended Dosage: 50-600 mg

Description: Important for cell energy production via mitochondria; synergizes with B vitamins in energy production from glucose; has a unique antioxidant effect against both water and fat-soluble free radicals.

B Complex Vitamins:

A group of eight vitamins, required in very small amounts to convert fat, protein and carbohydrates to energy. Most B vitamins we get plenty naturally through our food sources, because of the small amounts needed. You may add B-1 (Thiamin), B-3 (Niacin), B-12, and Folic acid to your supplement intake.

Vitamin B-3 (Niacin):

Niacin produces the basis of a powerful antioxidant system to protect most cells from the damaging effects of highly reactive molecules called free radicals. Niacin may prevent heart attacks, lower blood cholesterol and blood fat levels, while increasing high-density lipoprotein (the desirable form of cholesterol).

Vitamin B-12 (Pyridoxal Phosphate):

Recommended Dosage: 500-2000 mcg daily. Description: Vitamin B-12 helps to oxidize certain fatty acids and it supports the maintenance of healthy nerves. Mental deterioration including senility, dementia, and depression may respond to extra B-12. It also helps in the treatment of fatigue and age-related decline in energy level. Alzheimer's patients often have low B-12 levels.

Folic Acid:

Folic acid is a member of the B-complex family. Folic acid is essential for cell division. Folic acid deficiency is one of the most common vitamin deficiencies worldwide. Deficiency symptoms include fatigue, mental disturbances, and growth problems.

Gingko Biloba:

Recommended Dosage: 40-80 mg daily.

Description: A substance derived from gingko leaves, is truly remarkable. It expands the diameter of our blood vessels and arteries. It fights off damage from free radicals in the brain and throughout the body. Ginkgo increases brain blood flow which improves memory. Need to be taken consistently for 3 months to notice effects and then continued to maintain the effects. CAUTION: Consult a medical doctor before using if you have a tendency to bleed easily or have high blood pressure.

Flexseed Oil:

Recommended Dosage: 1-2 tablespoons daily with food and vitamin E.

Description: Contains more than 25 anti-aging compound. Has the highest omega-3 oil content in nature.

Phosphatidylserine (PS):

Recommended Dosage: 100 mg, 3 times daily.

Description: A major fat subtype in the brain that keeps nerve cell membranes intact yet fluid. Nutritional deficiencies in B-12, folate, SAM or essential fatty acids leads to decreased brain levels of PS, causing low acetylcholine levels, memory problems, and depression. PS is an expensive supplement and may not be worth the investment.

Lecithin (Phosphatidylcholine):

Recommended Dosage: 5-10 grams of 90% PC-lecithin.

Description: Lecithin is a substance that converts into the primary neurotransmitter acetycholine and also has been shown to improve memory. Take with the B complex vitamin group.

DHEA:

DHEA, a natural precursor to estrogen and testosterone, has been publicized as a supplement to boost memory. DHEA levels do decrease with age, and low DHEA has been associated with illnesses such as diabetes, osteoporosis, and dementia.

DMEA (Dimethylaminoethanol):

Recommended Dosage: 100-1000 mg daily; variable individual response.

   Description: Another exciting brain product. A source of choline that is storable in limitless amounts in brain neurons. It tends to disappear as we age. DMAE increases IQ, attention span, and ability to learn and recall. It helps to correct hyperactivity (attention disorder). DMAE can have a stimulating effect different from caffeine. There are studies that show DMAE solves acute problems of seniors: inability to pay attention (key to learning and memory) and to concentrate on writing and studying.

CHAPTER FOUR
AGING AND MEMORY

Weapons for Fighting Depression

Everybody Forgets

Sharpen your Memory Power

Senility and Dementia

Depression: When to get help

When do I Worry?

AGING AND MEMORY

As we grow older, our short-term memory functions and the speed of recall often relapse with aging. Short-term memory, is generally thought of as the number of information items that can be held in memory for a brief period of time. Though annoying, forgetfulness need not be debilitating. We know that serious memory loss is not an inevitable consequence of aging. Memory serves as the bases of learning. Because memory is selective, it will usually serve the learning process throughout life: Though perhaps slower to learn, an older person can be more accurate. It seems clear that the mental faculties of most older people remain functioning when exercised and challenged by a obligation to lifelong learning and activity. Furthermore, research suggests that people may be developed to partially retrieve their mental function apparently lost during aging. While it is true that older people are at increased risk for a dementia, such as Alzheimer's disease, the risk is much lower then most people might think.

Forgetfulness can be generated by depression, by the use of alcohol, tranquilizers and sleeping pills, by certain drug interactions and by any factor that decreases the supply of oxygen to the brain.

Stress and depression often are silent partners. To understand how stress affects our memory, we need to look at what happens when we feel stress. When we become stressed our heart rate increases, senses are heightened, blood flow to extremities are restricted and blood flow to the brain is increased. When we become stressed, we often go into a depressive mood. In fact, the same hormone that appears to dampen memory during stress also floods the brain when you feel depressed, and the feeling that go along with depression can severely block memory.

When we are depressed, it is harder for us to pay attention and concentrate. In fact, being more distracted is one of the symptoms of a depressed mood. Depression almost always makes everything in the brain work much more slowly. When you are feeling down, do not worry about your memory. It is good to keep in mind that when you are depressed you are more likely to be distracted and less able to concentrate. When you are depressed it will always take you more time to recall memories, and it becomes much harder to retain new information. A person who is stressed or under depression may only be able to recall something for a minute or two and then instantly forget.

Some people might face major depression, which is an illness in which the feelings of depression or sadness become overwhelming. This major depression may last for weeks or months. Serious depression may require counseling and medications. Major depression makes a person feel listlessness, hopelessness, and Anxiety. People who go through this type of depression often complain of difficulty of concentration and of memory problems. If you are just feeling down, you may find that the depressing mood will pass in hours-and when it does, it will be easier for you to regain your concentration.

Weapons for Fighting Depression

Take a Mental Break: When we are blue, we tend to mope and that is no time to put your memory to the test. If you forget something like calling a family member or picking up a gallon of milk, you might start believing that you are having memory problems and allow yourself to become more depressed. So even if you generally have a good memory, allow yourself to rely on lists and notes when you are feeling depressed. Then when you get past the blue mood, you can return confidently back to your memory.

Turning Negatives into Positives: When you find yourself making negative comments about others or yourself, try to catch yourself right away and take the time to think of a more positive way to say what you feel. What we tell ourselves is generally what we believe, so to say "I can't", will almost always guarantee a bad outcome. When we speak bad about other people, we present ourselves as negative minded and others most likely will treat us as such. A person who is always speaking positive, is usually a positive person and these people are always a joy to be around.

Exercise: Walking, running, and other exercises will help enhance memory. When you allow your heart rate to raise from aerobic exercise, it increases the blood and oxygen levels to go up in the brain. Doing any aerobic exercise for at least 20 minutes a day, three times a week, can enhance our ability to recall.

Laughter as Medicine: Laughter is one of the best medicines for depression and memory problems. Try to take time to read the cartoons, a funny book, go to a comedy club, or watch a funny program on television. Finding something funny to laugh about is the best way to enhance your mood and your memory.

Avoid Smoking: There is an association with Down's syndrome and thyroid disease. Smoking a pack of cigarettes a day expands the possibility of developing Alzheimer's disease.

Taking Care of Emotional Needs and Stress: Depression is a feeling of over-whelming sadness and causes anxiety. We all have had the feeling of anxiety. The feeling of having butterflies in our stomach is often how we might describe how anxiety feels within us. Anxiety affects our memory ability in the same way it influences our other performances. Anxiety often causes us to be more distracted. When we are distracted, we have a difficult time remembering things. Anxiety is a normal feeling but often is enhanced when we are depressed.

Depression causes us to have the inability to feel pleasure, have a loss of appetite, causing weight issues, excessive guilt, and depression can interfere with our ability to concentrate.

Keep Mental Active: When you stay mentally active, or when you exercise, your brain produces endorphins. Endorphins are produced by the body in response to pain, stress and emotions. Often people who run long distances, speak about the "high" they get from these endorphins. The endorphins give them the extra strength to go a little bit further. Endorphins bind to specific sites in the brain associated with pain perception and sedation. They may also assist in memory, learning, sexual drive, and regulation of body temperature.

Eat Wisely: See chapter: Food and Memory

Everybody Forgets

Everybody forgets-often when we do we might feel embarrassed which can cause anxiety, or it can turn out to be humorous. It is just part of being human. Chances are, whoever you are, you have forgotten something you wish you'd remembered. All of us forget and it has nothing to do with our age. Concerns about how well we remember, has no age limit. Memory is on the minds of the young and the old. It seems that even younger people feel they can increase their memory, and other younger people worry they are losing their memory. It is just part of being human. Weather you are 10 or 110, you can and will lose a book, your glasses, the house keys, or you might have a hard time recalling someone's name.

It is true that memory does seem to worsen with age. According to a 1995 survey, 80 percent of people age 35 and older reported having at least some problems with memory or concentration. This might have a lot to do with how many balls we are trying to juggle. Multi-tasking seem to be one of the biggest problems facing our memory. Work, family, bills, Emails, ect. can cause our attention to be stretched to it's limit and can certainly cause depression and anxiety.

By age 45, 56 percent of Americans adults say they habitually lose things and 45 percent say they have trouble recalling familiar names, according to a survey commissioned by the Charles A. Dana Foundation.

Just because we know that our memory ability will deteriorate as we age, it does not mean we are facing senility or dementia. Most memory loss is not severe. With the exception of serious neurological problems like Alzheimer's disease.

A person in their early 20's, for instance, might be able to recall seven to ten digits of a phone number. That same person at the age of 60 may only be able to recall six to eight numbers. You might notice that there really isn't anything incredibly disturbing about the difference between the age gaps.

Sharpen Your Memory Power

Shopping for Memory: Here is an easy way to sharpen your memory power. The next time you go to the grocery store, instead of counting on your grocery list, try to memorize it by using a memory technique.

When you do this regularly, you will find that you can memorize more and more things. Not just at the store but at home and in the office.

Turn off the Telly: Watching the television is the perfect way to turn your brain off. There is a good reason why we call the television the boob tube. Watching the television takes away all the need to use our brain or our memory. We do not have to use our creativity or logic. When we are watching television, we are killing our memory abilities.

I Love the Telly: If you love watching the television, and can not seem to be able to pull yourself away. Try to use it as a memory tool. During commercials, notice if the commercial uses names, such as Dr. so and so, or a model or actress. Make a point to memorize the persons name and their face. Then the next time you see the commercial, see if you can recall the name of the person used in the commercial before they show their name.

If you watch educational shows about history or autobiography, take small notes during the program and in a few days, see if you can recall the information you wrote down. You might be surprised on how much more of the program you can recall above and beyond the notes.

Reading Minds: Why not pick up the latest best-seller and lose yourself in fiction, mystery, or romance? Reading is a proven brain booster that helps enhance language skills while keeping your mind and memory strong. How-to and self help books are great books to add to your life. Not only will you help your mind, you might help your education, emotions, or other abilities as well.

Having Cross Words: Crossword puzzles are a great way to enhance your mind. Your brain is forced to think and organize thoughts. Which helps with the way you organize thoughts and memories. The twisted logic behind these puzzles teach your brain to be more creative. Crossword puzzles and other puzzles exercises the brain cells involved in word retrieval, vocabulary, and comprehension.

Hind and Words: Writing a letter to a loved one once a week is the perfect way to clarify thoughts and enhance memory and logic. Even if your not a great author, take the time to read over your letter, correcting spelling. Be creative by finding other words that mean the same thing. Just remember that every time you pick up the pen or your computer to create an E-mail, instead of the telephone, you're improving your mind and memory.

Mind Your Numbers: The next time you have a math problem, do not pick up the calculator. Pick up the pen and paper. These days no one can count money or do simple math in their heads. But doing math without a calculator creates logic and expands our ability to think and recall.

Senility and Dementia

Senility (Senile dementia):

Senility is memory loss associated with aging. This experience usually begins with the loss of short-term memory and hampers the ability to process new information quickly. Being able to remember past events also seem to slow down. The brain makes less neurotransmitters, which are chemicals required to relay nerve impulses, associated to short-term memory as it ages.

People who appear to be suffering from senile dementia and forgetfulness may experience nutritional deficiencies, including vitamin B-12 deficiency due to insufficient absorption. The uptake of this vitamin relapses with age, especially in those with stomach troubles. Injection of vitamin B-12 or taking large doses in tablet form is a preventive measure.

Forgetfulness, learning difficulties, and problems recalling new things can usually be generated by over-medication. Memory loss is also worsened by drugs blocking the formation of the neurotransmitters. Other possible difficulties of forgetfulness include high fever, minor head injuries, depression, loneliness, and boredom. Consult a specialist in geriatrics for mental changes in older people. To combat senility, exercise the brain by keeping mentally active and avoid drugs that characteristically provoke a dry mouth because this class of drugs may interfere with neurotransmitters. NEVER stop taking medication prescribed to you from your physician without seeking his or her advice.

Dementia (Senile psychosis):

A permanent mental deterioration that characterizes decreased mental functioning. Psychiatrists specify five indicators of senile psychosis: impairment of judgment, memory, orientation, intellectual functioning and changeable emotional response. General mental deterioration often occurs after the age of 70 with a gradual onset. Typically dementia brings short-term memory lapses, loss of interest in life, fitful sleep, mood swings, and confusion.

Certain illnesses can create apparent senility: heavy metal poisoning, alcoholism, high fever due to infections, disorders of the liver and kidney, hormonal imbalances.

Even though senility is not in most people's future, the brain is affected by aging in less dramatic ways. After age 45, it does take longer to recall things. It also takes the brain longer to digest new information. Older people can still learn, but they need more time than younger people.

Neurologists have observed that, as people age, some alterations in the brain make it more difficult to concentrate and recall recent memories, such as what was for supper yesterday. But long-term memories are relatively untouched.

But even though changes in the brain may be accountable for some memory loss, the physical changes that occur in general aging are primarily slight.

DEPRESSION
When To Get Help

If you have at least five of the following symptoms for two weeks or more, you may have depression and should see your physician as soon as possible:

1. Depressed mood most of the time.
2. Lack of interest in pleasure or all activities.
3. Unintentional change in weight over a month.
4. Significant expand or decrease in appetite.

5. Insomnia or over sleeping nearly every day.
6. Constant fatigue and loss of energy.
7. Feeling worthlessness or excessive/inappropriate guilt.
8. Lack of ability to think or concentrate.
9. Recurrent thoughts of death or suicide.

DEPRESSION
When To Get Help

If you have at least five of the following symptoms for two weeks or more, you may have depression and should see your physician as soon as possible:
1. Depressed mood most of the time.
2. Lack of interest in pleasure or all activities.
3. Unintentional change in weight over a month.
4. Significant expand or decrease in appetite.
5. Insomnia or over sleeping nearly every day.
6. Constant fatigue and loss of energy.
7. Feeling worthlessness or excessive/inappropriate guilt.
8. Lack of ability to think or concentrate.
9. Recurrent thoughts of death or suicide.

WHEN DO I WORRY?
My Memory is Getting Really Bad

If you notice that your memory or the memory of a loved one is getting really deficient and you worry there may be something seriously wrong:
1. Getting lost while driving a familiar route.
2. Forgetting important appointments.
3. Telling the same stories repeatedly during a single conversation.
4. Being unable to manage simple finances-like balancing the checkbook when you did not have problems before.
5. A sudden change in artistic or musical abilities.

If you have experienced any of these problems, or if you are losing memory to such a degree that it is getting impossible to function, then you need to check with your physician.

A physical problem-as well as age, can contribute to memory loss, and sometimes that problem is treatable or reversible.

There are more than 70 conditions that can introduce memory problems or worsen memory loss. The conditions include some that you might expect and many that you would not. From hearing loss, vision problems, stress to high blood pressure and depression. If you have been more distracted than usual, ask your physician for a complete physical examination before you jump to the conclusion that your mind is failing you.

Check your medications. Distractibility, poor attention, and memory problems can be side effects of drugs like tranquilizers and antidepressants. Ask your physician if your prescription or over the counter medications may be impairing your memory.

CHAPTER FIVE
THREE SIMPLE MEMORY
TECHNIQUES

The Peg Memory Technique

The Train Memory Technique

The LOCI Memory Technique

The Peg Memory Technique

The Peg Memory Technique, pairs the numbers one to ten with an imagined object. The number and the object or word rhymes, making them easy to remember.

1. One—Bun
2. Two—Tool
3. Three—Tree
4. Four—Door
5. Five—Hive
6. Six—Sticks
7. Seven—Heaven
8. Eight—Gate
9. Nine—Vine
10. Ten—Hen

Once you memorize the word or object that matches up with the number, you will be ready to begin using this memory technique.

To practice this technique. I am going to use the Seven dwarfs from Snow White. I can remember up to ten items or use the technique to memorize seven or less items.

Seven Dwarfs from Snow White

1. Doc
2. Grumpy
3. Sneezy
4. Sleepy
5. Bashful
6. Happy
7. Dopey

Now I will list the Peg Memory words alongside of each of the Dwarfs names. Doing this, we will be able to connect the two words together.

Bun—Doc
Tool—Grumpy
Tree—Sneezy
Door—Sleepy
Hive—Bashful
Sticks—Happy

Heaven—Dopey

Now to complete this memory technique, we need to create a story by putting the two words together to form a sentence or story. This is what I came up with:

1. Bun/Doc: I see a foot long subway bun cut open on the doctors table as he pulls out the pickles. It seems like the doc has to do surgery on every sandwich he orders, just to get the pickles out.

2. Tool/Grumpy: The grumpy carpenter nails in a nail and it bends. The next nail goes in crooked. Now he is really grumpy and he slams his tools to the floor out of frustration.

3. Tree/Sneezy: In my back yard I have many flowering trees. There are many colors and nice smells, but the pollen from all the trees causes me to be sneezy.

4. Door/Sleepy: At night as you tuck your child in, you might see the sleepy eyes, but notice how wide awake the child becomes the moment you try to shut the door completely. So you leave the door slightly ajar for your sleepy child.

5. Hive/Bashful: You see a bear being real bashful when he approaches a bee hive. You can tell that this bear has been stung a few times in his life. Even though he might be bashful toward approaching the hive, you know he will get the honey.

6. Sticks/Happy: Have you ever noticed that you can buy your young children expensive toys but with their imagination they can be happier with two sticks. The sticks are mighty swords that help the child protect their pirate ship. Just remember that kids can be happy with simple sticks.

7. Heaven/Dopey: Who will make it to heaven? Will a child if it dies young? How about someone who is retarded? If this is true, I should make it. I am a little dopey. At least all of my friends think so.

Now imagine that you want to use it as a way to remember things you need to do during the day. Such as: Pay the bills, take the car to the shop, buy a new pair of shoes, or mail some letters.

I would memorize it like this: I would visualize the bills rolled up like a hot dog and place them in a bun as I cover them with mustard. I might picture a pair of shoes tied together by the shoestrings hanging off a branch of a tree. The mail I would see stuck in the crack of the door to my house, half sticking out.

This technique is very simple to learn and can be used in so many different ways that it is one of my favorites to teach to both young and old alike.

The Train Memory Technique

The train Memory Technique is a fun memory system that can be used to memorize short amount of memory. Such as: "honey-do" lists, grocery lists, or you can use it in conjunction with other memory techniques that you might want to break down into smaller sections.

To learn this memory technique I am going to make a list of six "memory tools" that we might use to help us with our daily memory.

Memory Tools

> To-Do List
> Medication Box
> Address Book
> Calendar
> Note Pad
> Organizer

Now that we have the list that we want to remember. Let's imagine that we want to remember this list in numeric order as well.

This is how the Train Memory Technique will work. First we will create a train using six train cars. Listed below is the name of the train cars and the order that I will have them connected. I want you to memorize and picture each car as if you are the one placing them together on the train track.

> Steam Engine
> The Coal Car
> The Passenger Car
> The Flat Car
> The Box Car
> The Little Red Caboose

Steam Engine/Coal Car/Passenger/Flat Car/Box car/Caboose

Now as you look at the words of how the train is set up. Imagine that you can see each car in detail. On the Engine, picture the smoke stack. On the coal car. Visualize seeing the coal piled high out the top. In the passenger car. Notice the windows where the passengers are looking out and waving good bye to their family and friends. Imagine the flat car being used to carry large items like trucks and tractors. When you picture the box car. Think of the hobo's running to the slidding doors, and jumping in for a free ride. When you get to the little red caboose. Visualize how the presidents use to stand on the back of these trains as they went through towns. How the back of the caboose was covered with the red, white and blue ribbons.

Now for us to memorize the list of memory tools we need to create a story in our minds to attach the items to the train: Below are the stories I used:

1. Engine/To-do list: I visualize the engineer looking at the side of the cabin to check the to-do list before he gets started. First shovel coal in box. Second, build up steam. Third, release the break.

2. Coal car/Medication box: First I want to remind you what a medication box is. It is a plastic organizer that is usually divided up into small compartments marked each with a day of the week. Thus, a reminder of which pill to take on which day. I would visualize the coal car overflowing with pills instead of coal.

3. Passenger car/Address book: I would think of all the people riding in the passenger car who pull out their address book to find the addresses of everyone they will send a postcard to, since the ride allows them time.

4. Flat car/Calendar: I see that there was no trucks or tractors to put on the flat car this trip. Instead there is a big billboard that has a calendar of May and mothers day is circled. Next to the calendar is a slogan for a card company that says: "Don't forget mom".

5. Box car/Note pad: In the box car is cases and cases of note pads being shipped to a big retailer. The hobo opens one of the cases and is disappointed that there is nothing to eat. But he has an idea. He rips the pages out of a few note pads and start a small fire. While sitting next to the fire he flips open a note pad and starts writing notes which he plans on making into a book one day.

6. Caboose/Organizer: I don't know what the guy in the caboose is called. All I know is that he is usually the one waving at everyone as the train goes through town. He is also the one who has the little pocket watch in his hand. He must be the organizer of the train. Each time he steps into the caboose he opens his organizer and writes down what time the train leaves, when it arrives at each location, and how many boxes of note pads there are in the box car.

Now, if you think of your train in this memory technique, you should be able to recall in what order the train cars are connected. Then if you think of each car individually, you should be able to recall what "memory tool" we placed on each train car. Doing this will help you remember the memory tools as well as what order they should be in.

This memory technique can be used in many ways. If you practice you will be able to use it in your everyday life. one example would be remembering a short grocery list. Here is my shopping list:

Cookies
Chip
Soup
Ice Cream
Soda
M&M Candy

Now what we would do is visualize the engineer driving the train while eating cookies. The coal car filled overflowing with nacho chips instead of coal. The passengers would all be sitting at tables eating soup as they look out the window watching the scenery pass by. The flat car would have the worlds largest scoop of ice cream on it, and I see it melting and dripping off the sides. The box car would be filled with cases of my favorite soda, and I might add a hobo riding in there, sitting on a few cases as he guzzles a few cans down. The last car. The caboose. I might imagine how the presidents use to stand on the "back porch" of the caboose campaigning. But instead of a president, I might visualize the red and green M&M guys saying: "Pick me as your favorite color"I And waving at the crowds as the train passes through each town.

LOCI Memory Technique

The Greeks are credited for coming up with this memory technique. The name: "Loci", has the meaning: "Mental walk". The technique uses locations to help you store things in your memory. The way it works is first you decide on a familiar place that you can visualize in your head. It can be your office, your living room, the bedroom, your church, or even a baseball stadium.

I am first going to use the baseball stadium for an example. Let's first think of the positions available to the baseball players:

> Pitcher
> Catcher
> First Base
> Second Base
> Third Base
> Shortstop
> Left field
> Center Field
> Right Field

Do not just look at the words. In your head I want you to visualize each playing position. Get the whole baseball diamond in your mind and imagine that you are at bat.

Directly in front of you is the pitcher. The first baseman is off to your right. Third baseman is there on your left. Behind the pitcher you see the second baseman and behind him, way out deep is the center field.

Now let's create a grocery list of things we need to pick up from the store:

Lemons	Corn
Hot dogs	Club soda
Wild rice	Ice cream
Grapes	cigarettes
Potatos	

When your thinking of the ball players, you want to start with the player closest to you, the batter, and work your way out.

The catcher would be first, then the pitcher, next you will start on the right which will be first base, then second base, short stop, third base.

In the out field we will do the same by starting on the right side of the field. We have the right field, the center field, and then last is the left field.

The reason we do this is because sometimes we might have to remember lists of things in a particular order. 1, 2, 3, 4, ect. and we want to have a set pattern to direct our positions on the field. In the example I am giving; a grocery list, there is no special order. So in cases like this. We can place the items in the spots that we like best.

This is how I would remember the grocery list:

I look back at the pitcher and I notice he is making sour faces at me. Then I realize it isn't me. He has a lemon hidden in his glove and he keeps taking a bite. He must be trying to stop chewing tobacco. (Lemons)

The pitcher is really tall and skinny, I see him as a corn cob, bright yellow with legs sticking out the end. (com)

The first player is blind/and he has a seeing eye dog. I feel really sorry for the dog because there is no water for him and he is drooling. I can tell he is a very hot dog. (Hot Dogs)

The guy at second is dressed in a fancy suit. He has a silk tie and alligator shoes. He doesn't belong here. He belongs to a country club where he can drink soda. (Club Soda)

The short stop has a fur jump suit on and looks like a caveman. His hair is matted and standing straight up. He looks like a wild man. (Wild rice)

Third baseman looks really bored. He's standing there eating a ice cream. He's holding it in his left hand because he has a glove on his right. The ice cream is melting all over his fingers and he keeps trying to lick it clean but it is really messy. He has ice cream all over his mouth, his uniform and some even dripped on his shoes. He looks over at first base at the seeing eye dog thinking that any minute, the dog is going to come running over and attack him. (Ice Cream)

Right field is a bunch of grapes. He was in commercial about underwear but then he got a new contract to play baseball. Usually the commercials recruit stars and make them actors. This time the Grape man was a commercial star and became an athlete. (Grapes)

Center field is a disgrace to the team. All these athletes are exercising and staying in shape and here this guy is out there dressed like a cowboy, with his cowboy boots, his ten gallon hat, and smoking a cigarette. Wait a minute. I know him. He was the guy on all the billboards advertising the cigarettes, (cigarettes)

Left field has a spade, a bushel basket and a pile of dirt next to him. I think he is looking for his family. When he turns to look at me, I notice his nose is where his eye should be, his lips are where his ear is suppose to be. What is going on here? His head looks like a Mr. Potato head. (Potatoes)

The loci technique can be used in any situation. You can use your bedroom by standing at the door and scan your room from right to left. In your mind you should visualize only the big objects of your room. The dresser, the night stand, the bed, the shelf. But clear out all the little stuff that you have laying around.

Let's say the dresser is on the right wall. The night stand is on the right of the bed which is directly in front of you. Then on the left wall, lets say there is a shelf next to a window.

Now let's put our grocery list in the room. Starting on the right we have the dresser. I want you to visualize two lemons and two corn cobs sitting on the dresser, reflecting the bright yellow in the mirror.

On the night stand is a half eaten hot dog and a glass of club soda that we must have left there from last night.

On the bed is a bed spread that your grandma made you years ago. It's brown and it reminds you of wild rice. On the pillow cases is printed ice cream cones with brown cones. At least it matches the blanket.

On the shelf is the perfume that you loved until your friends told you that you smelled like a bunch of grapes. Next to that cheap grape smelling perfume is the pack of cigarettes that your friend left in your room. You should have told them not to smoke in your room. Now you can smell the stench in the curtains.

Looking out the window you see your neighbor coming in with his groceries. Sticking out the top of his grocery bag is potatoes. That reminds you that you need a few potatoes yourself.

Do you see how you can use this technique in any room you can possibly think of? I know a preacher that will stand in his church before giving a sermon and plant memory items to help him preach without looking at his notes. He might put a "ship in a bottle" on the front pew to remind him of Noahs ark. An Olympic athlete against the right wall to remind him of the story of the talents. He might place two stone tablets next to a cross on the back wall to help him recall his plan to talk about "Grace and the Law".

This memory technique is great for people who want to give speeches without notes. That is how the Greek rulers would give their speeches for hours at a time and not look at one written note.

CHAPTER SIX
THE ARROW AND EGG
MEMORY TECHNIQUE

The Ten Commandments

The Story Telling Technique

Arrow and Egg Memory Technique

The Arrow and Egg memory technique is a sensational memory technique that works great for short lists or as a secondary tool to other memory techniques.

Listed below are the numbers one through zero. Beside each of the numbers are words that will represent that number:

1. Arrow
2. Swan
3. Clover
4. Golf flag
5. Hook
6. Cherry Bomb
7. Fiddler
8. Snowman
9. Long Tail Cat
0. Egg

Take notice how each word describes the number. For example, if you look closely at the one (1), you will find that it resembles an arrow pointing up.

Notice how the two (2) looks like a swan. If you draw a little beak on the top curve of the two, you will see the swan better.

You can associate the three (3) to a lucky three leaf clover. But if you were to draw a three and add another leaf and a stem, you would have a 3 leaf clover.

The four (4) looks like a golf flag without any additional drawing, but I extend the vertical line of the four to make the flag "pole" a little longer and then I would draw a circle around the base of the pole to make it look as though it is planted in a hole.

If you remove the top horizontal line of the five (5), you will have what looks like a fish hook. Or, if you leave the horizontal line and turn the five on it's side it looks like one of those hooks you screw into the wall to hang your tea cups on.

Six (6) is the cherry bomb because as a kid I used to love to buy them at the fourth of July fireworks display. The circle of the six looks like the cherry bomb and the line coming out the top is the fuse that you would light with a match.

Seven (7) might be your most difficult to visualize. But if you would draw a little circle for a head where the horizontal and vertical lines meet and than draw another line off of the vertical line for another leg, you would see a person playing a fiddle. I usually will stand up with my legs together, extent my left arm straight out, then bring my right arm across my body as if I was going to play a violin or fiddle. Picturing what my body looks like in this position. It looks like the number 7.

Eight (8) is the simplest one to see. I like to draw a top hat on the first circle to make it look more like Frosty the snowman.

Nine (9) is often hard for some people to see the cat. If you would imagine a cat sitting in the window with his back toward you and the tail is curled down. Then you might see him. I usually draw a little head on top of the circle of the 9, and put little ears on the head that I drew. This usually makes it easier for everyone to visualize the cat with the long tail.

Zero (0) is self explanatory. The important thing to remember about the zero is that it represents the number ten (10).

*A Helpful Hint:

Write 1-0 on a scrap piece of paper and draw the representing picture out of each number and secure each picture in your mind before going any further.

Arrow and Egg Memory Technique
And
The Ten Commandments

Most people can not recall more than a few of the Commandments. I have met only a very few who knew all ten, and none of them could recall them in order or very quickly.

By using the Arrow and Egg technique, you will find that memorizing the Ten Commandments will be very simple and best of all, it is fun. Now let's begin by showing you how to incorporate the Arrow and Egg memory system to the Ten Commandments.

The Ten Commandments

(Simplified)

We have only one God.
Do not worship idols.
Do not use Gods' name in vain.
Keep the Sabbath holy.
Honor your mother and Father.

Do not murder.
Do not commit adultery.
Do not steal.
Do not lie on others.
Do not covet your neighbors' wife or stuff.

Story Telling Memory Technique

Story telling memory is a useful memory technique that is often combined with other memory programs. In all the memory systems that we will share in this book, you will be using the story telling system simultaneously with the others. You will see how this will work as you go. But first let me explain how the story telling system works.

An example of story telling would best be used if you were in need to remember a license plate number of a hit and run driver. Let's just say that a car ran into your brand new car. You see the license plate number as it speeds away. NM120. You could repeat it over and over in hopes that you will not forget (like we do with flash cards in math or other traditional memory habits), but a better way would be to create a "story". It does not have to be long. It can be something very simple, such as: "New Mexico summers get as hot as 120°". Short, simple and easy to retain.

The more creative you are, the better you will remember. An important thing to point out. If your story is unusual, creative and fictional, you will recall it better. Now let's look at how you will incorporate the Arrow and Egg Technique and the Story Telling Technique together.

Let's start off with the Ten Commandments. We already simplified the Commandments into easy to read sentences, but now let's take it one step further. Let's make them as simple as one word. And we will call this one word, our "keyword".

The Ten Commandments as Keywords

We have only one God—God
Do not worship idols—Idols
Do not use Gods' name in vain—Name
Keep the Sabbath holy—Sabbath
Honor your mother and father—Mother and Father
Do not murder—Murder

Do not commit adultery—Adultery
Do not steal—Steal
Do not lie on others—Lie
Do not covet your neighbors' wife and stuff—Covet

Now that we have our keywords for each of the Commandments, we will list them next to our symbols:

1. Arrow—God
2. Swan—Idols
3. Clover—Name
4. Golf Flag—Sabbath
5. Hook—Mother and Father
6. Cherry Bomb—Murder
7. Fiddler—Adultery
8. Snowman—Steal
9. Long Tail Cat—Lie
0. Egg—Covet

Now what we want to do is create a story that will include the symbol and the commandment keyword. I have created my own stories for examples. You might use these stories or create your own:

1. (Arrow/God) The first one is the arrow and God. What I want you to do is take your index finger and hold it up in front of you. Point to the sky and say: "We have only one God". The finger represents the arrow pointing to heaven and it represents the one (1) for the first Commandment.

2. (Swan/Idols) Since we are talking about the Ten Commandments, let's think of Moses coming down the side of the mountain carrying the tablets. When he reaches the bottom he finds the people bowing down to a golden calf. In our associating thinking, let's make the idol a golden swan.

3. (Clover/Name) The Christians claim that God has three names. Father, Son, and Holy Spirit. Each name represents God. Visualize each leaf of the three leaf clover having a name written on it. You now have three leaves, with three names. Remember that you will not use Gods' name in vain.

4. (Golf Flag/Sabbath) When do people play golf? Usually on the weekends. Well, they should not, because they should be keeping the Sabbath.

5. (Hook/Mother and Father) Your mom and dad hooked up to make you, so you should honor your mother and father for making you.

6. (Cherry Bomb/Murder) If you were to make a pipe bomb and set it off in a crowded area, it would kill people. Do not Murder.

7. (Fiddler/Adultery) A fiddler is mostly used in country music. Country music is more often than not, talking about cheating on someone. Do not commit adultery.

8. (Snowman/Steal) Frosty the snowman had a magic hat. Every time the hat was on Frostys' head, he would come alive. But the evil old man was always stealing the hat and than the kids would get the hat back and put it on Frostys' head, and Frosty would come back alive. But that evil man would just steal it again. Do not steal.

9. (Long Tail Cat/Lie) What does a cat do all day long? That's right, it lies around. Lazy cat. Do not Lie.

10. (Egg/Covet) Remember the golden swan? Now I have a golden egg and it is worth 1 million dollars. I bet you wish you could have it. Well, do not covet my golden egg.

CHAPTER SEVEN
THE INFINITY MEMORY
TECHNIQUE

Memorizing the Presidents

What are Subtitles?

The Infinity Memory System

The infinity memory system receives its name because unlike the other memory techniques you have learned so far, there is no end to what you can remember.

With the infinity system you can memorize as little as two or three items, a group of ten (such as the Ten Commandments), or as you will see, the four Gospels with little effort.

To learn this technique, we have three easy steps. The first step might remind you of the Arrow and Egg system. In the Arrow and Egg system, you might recall that we associated the number to a symbol. In the Infinity Memory System, we will have letters of the alphabet represent the numbers.

The first step is listed below. Next to each number is a letter in which you should memorize each of the letters that are representing each of the numbers:

        1.= T
        2. = N
        3. = M
        4. = R
        5. = L
        6. = Sh
        7. = K
        8. = V
        9. = P
        0. = S

Each person will have their own unique way to "connect" or memorize the letters to the numbers. But I would like to reflect back to the Story Telling System. Remember how we created "Memory Stories"? This technique is the most commonly used memory system because our minds love visual pictures. To help you memorize each letter and number I created memory stories and listed them below:

1. T = It takes one Touchdown to win the state title.

2. N = I have 2 nutty neighbors, named Nick and Nathan.

3. M = Three memorable mountains: Mount Rushmore, Mount Everest, and Mount Mckinley.

4. R = Four rustling wranglers played Russian Roulette at a Rio Grande Ranch.

5. L = Five lonely Ladies looking for Love.

6. Sh = There are six Shells to a half dozen eggs.

7. K = Seven lucky Kids ate cotton candy and caramel corn at the carnival.

8. V = I think of a V-8 engine.

9. P = There are nine Playing Position on a baseball team.

0. S = Zero Spells with a z, but Sounds like an S.

Adding Letters
(Step 2)

Part two of this three step process is adding a few new letters to what we have already learned. This should be very simple because the letters that we are adding are letters that make the same sound as the first set of letters that we have committed to memory. Here is an example: If you say T and then say D, you will notice that the sound is similar. You will also notice that your tongue touches the roof of your mouth when saying each of these letters. Memorize the added letters before continuing on with step 3.

> 1. =T and D
> 2. =N
> 3. =M
> 4. =R
> 5. =L
> 6. =Sh, Ch, J and G
> 7. =K and C (hard)
> 8. =V and F
> 9. =P and B
> 0. =S, Z, and C (soft)

*A Helpful Hint #1:

The letters representing number 6: Sh, Ch, J and G makes the same sound. AN example of this would be the words: Sheep, Cheap, Jeep and Geek.

There are two numbers that claim the letter C (number 7 and 0). This is because the C makes two sounds. The first C in number 7 is noticed in the words "caramel corn". This C sound is called a Hard C because it sounds like the letter K. The other C in number 0 is a Soft C because this C sounds like the letter S as in Mice, Rice, and Dice.

Take this time to write on a piece of paper the numbers 1-0 and see if you can remember the letters from memory. Be sure that you have them all memorized before moving on to the next and last step.

*A Helpful Hint #2:

Basically, you have to remember only the first letter to each number. The other letters make exactly the same sound. Try saying them out loud. Your mouth will do the same thing when you say P as it would if you say B. You will notice your mouth will pucker when you say each of these letters. With the letters T and D you will notice when you say the words utter and udder, you will hear the similarity. Now try saying: Chin, Jin, or Shin. These letters are from number 6, notice the different letters but the same sound?

Creating Word Foundation
(Third and last step)

So far you have memorized the foundation of putting the letters with numbers. Now we will give you a word foundation that will put you in the position to memorize a unlimited amount of knowledge. Once you complete this section, you will have the ability to memorize the four gospels of the New Testament in a matter of days.

The letters you have learned so far are consonants. Letters we did not use such a A, E, I, 0, U, Y are vowels. In this memory system we are going to add W and H to the list of vowels because they do not have a numeric value.

Now for the next step, we will be creating words out of letters that we have memorized. And to do this we will take the letter that represents a number and add vowels to it to create a word. Let's use 1 for an example: The letter we memorized for 1 is T. So if we were to add a couple of vowels to the letter T, we would create the word "tea".

Now let me give you a few words and see if you can figure out the number it represents: Write your answers on a scratch piece of paper.

Tea =	Wall =
Noah =	Shoe =
Me =	Key =
Hare =	Pay =

If your numbers went in order 1-8, then you answered the problem correctly. Often the word "hare" throw off the beginner because they might expect the first letter to be the "numeric valued letter", but we have to remember that H and W are counted in with the vowels. The same goes for wall. It is the L that carries the numeric value of 5. Now you might notice that wall has two L's. The rule is: If two letters "sounds" like a single letter, its value will be equal to one letter.

Now allow me to give you a list of words that you will use to have a numeric value. These words are never going to change. So you will want to dedicate them to your memory:

1. T = Tea
2. N = Noah
3. M = May
4. R = Hare
5. L = Wall
6. Sh = Shoe
7. K = Key
8. V = Wave
9. P = Pay
10. T & S or D & C = Dice

You will notice that when we got to the number 10, we had two letters. When you get into double digit numbers, you will have double letters. Each individual number will have its own letter.

*A Helpful Hint:

Let me take you back to the Peg Memory system. Do you recall how Bun was the word that represented the one? And Tool represented the two? These words we used are permanent. The same goes for this memory system. Often I have come across students who feel they can create better words than what is taught. Some try to use different words with every new thing they try to memorize. The outcome of everyone of these students so far has been a complete failure.

Memorizing the Presidents

Now that you have memorized the first ten words, we will put the memory system to the test. The words you memorized from this point on will be called your "keyword". For example: The keyword for 1 is Tea. The keyword for 2 is Noah, and so on. Now I want you to associate each of the keywords to the following U.S. Presidents:

> Washington
> Adams
> Jefferson
> Madison
> Monroe

I will give you an example of how this will be done. The first president of the United States was Washington.

> 1. (T) Keyword: Tea
> 1. Tea/Washington

The story that connect the keyword to the president will go like this:

The president wants some tea, I visualize a Chinese man with a pot full of tea leaves. He is scrubbing and washing them before serving the tea to the president.

Now what I want you to do is look at the first ten presidents that I listed below and see if you can create a story that corresponds the keyword to the president. Remember that the more creative the story is, the better we tend to remember it.

> (Tea) Washington
> (Noah) Adams
> (Me) Jefferson
> (Hare) Madison
> (Wall) Monroe
> (Shoe) Q. Adams
> (Key) Jackson
> (Wave) Van Buren
> (Pay) Harrison
> (Dice) Tyler

So how well did you do? Take a moment to test your memory by writing on a piece of paper 1-10 and see how many you are able to recall. Below I have listed the stories that I created for each president:

1. T (Tea) Washington—A Chinese man with a pot full of Tea leaves, scrubbing and washing them.

2. N (Noah) Adams—I think of Noah's ark going over A-dam.

3. M (Me) Jefferson—I visualize me and my son being invited to the oval office to talk with the president.
Jeff ing is slang for talking. So me and my son jeffing with the president.

4. R (Hare) Madison—When I am talking to the president, his toupee (hair piece) slides over a little and my son points and starts laughing. My son says: "look his hair is falling off." And I get mad-at-my-son.

5. L (Wall) Monroe—I see Marilyn Monroe sneaking around late at night and climbing the wall that surrounds the White House to see the president.

6. Sh (Shoe) Q. Adams—I visualize a pair of shoes tied to a wooden pool cue, floating down a river and going over A-Dam

7. K (Key) Jackson—Here I see Micheal Jackson standing on top of a black limousine with a hoard of people trying to get his autograph. He is celebrating because he just received the key to the city.

8. V (Wave) Van Buren—We are heading out to do some surfing, I'm driving my van onto the beach as the waves start brewing. The wave of water washes the sand from under my van and we become stuck.

9. P (Pay) Harrison—I am going to pay to get my hairy son a hair cut.

10. DC (Dice) Tyler—The president bought himself a classic 57' Chevy. He decides that it would not be complete unless he has a pair of those fuzzy dice to place on the rearview mirror. So he buys a pair of dice and "ties" it to the mirror.

*A Helpful Hint:

As you continue on to your next set of keywords: (11-19), you will notice that all the numbers (11-19) are associated with words that start with the letter T because 1 is represented by the T in the memory system. You will also notice that the numbers: 20-29 start with the letter N which represents the 2. An exception being made for the numbers 26 and 27.

Learning the next 20 keywords

Now that you have the idea of how this works, the next 20 words will be simple to retain, as long as you remember to only use the key letters that have a numeric value in the memory system.

11. = (TD) Toad
12. = (TN) Tin
13. = (TM) Tomb
14. = (TR) Tar
15. = (TL) Tail
16. = (TSh) Tissue
17. = (TK) Tack
18. = (TV) Taffy
19. = (TP) Tub
20. = (NS) Nose
21. = (NT) Net
22. = (NN) Nanny
23. = (NM) Name
24. = (NR) Near
25. = (NL) Nail
26. = (NSh) Wench
27. = (NK) Ink
28. = (NV) Navy
29. = (NP) Nap
30. = (MS) Mice

Memorizing the rest of the presidents

To memorize the presidents, you will continue to use the Infinity Memory System. Just like you did earlier when you memorized the first 10 presidents. I will list the presidents in order and then include stories to help you memorize them.

Washington
Adams
Jefferson
Madison

Monroe
Q. Adams
Jackson
Van Buren
Harrison
Tyler
Polk
Taylor
Fillmore
Pierce
Bucanan
Lincoln
Johnson
Grant
Hayes
Garfield

Stories for 11-20

TD (Toad) Polk—The president every year has a big Easter egg hunt, and then he has a big frog jumping contest. You enter your toad and he won't jump, so to get him started you polk the toad in the rear.

TN (Tin) Taylor—The president was an old red neck before becoming president. He lived in a mobile home, so when he became president he moved his old tin trailer (Taylor) behind the White House.

TM (Tomb) Fillmore—The old tomb or grave was dug six feet deep. After the casket was placed in the hole, people tossed dirt in, but it didn't cover the whole casket so they had to fillmore dirt in the tomb.

TR (Tar) Pierce—The road in front of the White House was being re-paved. The tar was spread over the top and the steam rollers with the square pegs on the roller was piercing (Pierce) the tar and flattening it.

TL (Tail) Buchanan—I visualize this big cannon (Buchanan) in front of the White House, and there is a long fuse sticking out the back which looks like a tail.

TSh (Tissue) Lincoln—Do you remember the yarn tissue box covers that you made in grade school? Now think of a tissue box cover made out of Lincoln logs.

TK (Tack) Johnson—Speaking of grade school. Did you ever play a prank where you stuck a thumb tack in someone's chair? Now think of doing that by placing a tack on the toilet seat in the John. (Johnson)

TV (Taffy) Grant—When you was a child, to get some candy, you needed to get permission. Now as an adult, you can grant yourself permission to eat taffy.

TP (Tub) Hayes—When the president was campaigning, he cut some hay in Nebraska. When he got in the tub to wash himself. He noticed that there was hay floating in the tub with him.

NS (Nose) Garfield—Garfield the cat had a big black nose and he was always sticking his nose into my food.

Presidents 21-30

Aurther
Cleveland
Harrison (Benjamin)
Cleveland
McKinley
Roosevelt (Theodore)
Taft
Wilson
Harding
Coolidge

Stories for 21-30

NT (Net) Aurther—I visualize a great castle replacing the White House. There is a moat running around the castle and there holding a net is King Auther trying to catch some fish.

NN (Nanny) Cleveland—Do you know the nanny that is on T.V. that talks funny? Well, she is from Cleveland.

NM (Name) Harrison—The president named his hairy son Benjamin.

NR (Near) Cleveland—When I told you that the nanny live in Cleveland. Actually she lives in the suburbs which is near Cleveland.

NL (Nail) McKinley—The president wanted to climb mount McKinley. He had to buy some of those nails that you drive into the rock to be able to reach the top of McKinley.

NSh (Wench) Roosevelt (Theodore)—You stop over to visit with the president. He invites you to afternoon tea. As you sit at the patio table the wench brings tea (Theodore) out to you in the rose (Roosevelt) garden.

NK (Ink) Taft—The president likes to sign his name with the old fashion quill. He has one that he dips into the taft which holds the ink. The taft is also known as an ink well.

NV (Navy) Wilson—I see these navy men on a ship playing soccer. One of them kicks the ball to hard and it lands in the ocean. When you look over the side of the ship at the ball, you read the word "Wilson" on the side of it.

NP (Nap) Harding—I hate taking a short nap during the day, because I sleep so hard (Harding) and I wake up more tired then if I would have stayed awake.

MS (Mice) Coolidge—The president wanted to get rid of all the mice. So he called the pied piper who played his flute and drew the mice up the staircase of a skyscraper. When he reached the 30th floor he drew the mice out on the cool ledge (coolidge) and had them jump to their death.

Presidents 31-43

Hoover
Roosevelt (Franklin)
Truman
Eisenhower
Kennedy
Johnson

Nixon
Ford
Carter
Reagan
Bush (George Sr.)
Clinton
Bush (George W.)

Stories for 31-43

31. MT (Maid) Hoover—The presidents maid uses a Hoover vacuum cleaner.

32. MN (Man) Roosevelt (Franklin)—When you think of a rose, you might not think of a man. When you think of a nickname "Rosie". You may not assume that it is a name for a great leader.

33. MM (Mom) Truman—I am glad my mom found a true man for a husband. Someone I am proud to call dad.

34. MR (Mare) Eisenhower—The beer company "Anheuser" (Eisenhower) reminds me of those big mares (horses) pulling the beer wagon.

35. ML (Mail) Kennedy—All the Kennedy men were known for being attractive men, one was voted most attractive male (mail).

36. MSh (Match) Johnson—I think of the name of the big company "Johnson and Johnson". The names Match each other.

37. MK (Make) Nixon—When you make something such as a cake, you have to mix in (Nixon) the ingredients.
38. MV (Move) Ford—When you move from one house to another, you need to rent a moving truck. Get the best. Move your stuff with a Ford.

39. MP (Map) Carter—Anytime I look at a map of Georgia, I think of president Carter.

40. RS (Rice) Reagan—I think of president Reagan back when he was an actor. They were celebrating a new movie release and all the people was throwing rice and taking pictures. It reminds me of a big wedding party.

41. RT (Rat) Bush Sr.—I see this big papa rat trying to hide in a bush, but the president saw it and called an exterminator.

42. RN (Rain) Clinton—The Republicans were glad to see the Clinton's reign (rain) end. But what about Hilary?

43. RM (Ram) Bush (George W.)—Some might say that the speed in which our military went into Iraq and Afganistan, president Bush "rammed" his way into those countries.

What are Subtitles?

When I started this memory system, I did not have to use anything but the keywords. But when I started studying the Bible, I found it difficult to create stories that was easy to associate to the name of the book. For an example, I do not personally know anyone by the name Luke. So for me to associate my memory stories to someone I don't know, was very difficult.

Then when I started studying the complete New Testament, I had a hard time memorizing and separating my stories in the books of John, I John, II John, and III John.

So I asked myself how I might be able to associate my memory stories to each book title. This is where my memory technique is a little different than most. What I did was created "subtitles" for each of the books.

A subtitle is simply a nickname that we learn to associate to each of the book titles. Every book in the New Testament received a subtitle or nick-name except Matthew. For some reason, since Matthew is the first book we learn, the need for a subtitle wasn't there.

Since we are just memorizing the four gospels of the New Testament, it should be very easy for you to remember the following subtitles:

Gospel Title:	Subtitle:
Matthew	Matthew
Mark	Friends name

Luke	A Doctor
John	Your dads name

When you start memorizing the gospels, I want you to remember to say the subtitle and then the keyword. An example of this would be like when we were memorizing the presidents.

You could have said: The presidents tea. The presidents noah. The president and me. The president's hare.

When we put the subtitle with the keyword like this, it plants the subject we are studying in our minds a little stronger. This helps us from getting confused on which book the chapter we were memorizing would be found in.

If we say the presidents hair (hare) was falling off, then we know our memory was about the president and not from a book in the Bible.

On each of the cover pages, and story telling page of each of the gospels I placed the subtitle to help us remember what each subtitle is. Once you memorize a complete book, you will never forget what it's subtitle is.

CHAPTER EIGHT
THE GOSPEL OF MATTHEW

(subtitle: Matthew)

The Outline of Matthew

The Story Telling System

The Review of Matthew

The book of Matthew

Chapter #

Genealogy of Jesus
The birth of Jesus
The baptism of Jesus
The temptation of Jesus
The fulfillment of the law
Praying and Fasting
Judging others
The healings
The calling of Matthew
Sending out the 12 disciples
Jesus and John the baptist
Lord of the Sabbath
The parables
John the baptist beheaded
Clean and unclean
Jesus predicts His death
The transfiguration
Greatest in heaven (children)
Divorce
Two blind men healed
Jesus at the temple
Whose Son is the Christ?
The seven woes
Signs of the end of the age
The parable of the talents
The Lord's supper
The crucifixion
The resurrection

The Gospel of Matthew
Story Telling System

1. The Genealogy of Jesus Keyword: Tea (T)

Genealogy to me is a family tree, or the family history. Usually you find a grandmother or grandfather telling stories of family history. So for the story telling memory visual that I use: My grandmother and I are sitting out on the front porch of her old home, it is a hot, lazy summer day. As we rock in the old rocking chairs, we drink a tall cold glass of tea, I listen to her tell me stories of my family history.

2. The Birth of Jesus Keyword: Noah (N)

The visual might be a bit crazy for some people but the important thing to remember about memory, is that the brain likes to be entertained. If it is exciting, or shocking, the brain will remember it better. Noah reminds me of the great flood. The first thing that a birth and a flood draws to thought is the breaking of the water when a woman is about to give birth.

3. The Baptism of Jesus Keyword: May (M)

May can be the start of spring in some areas. I think of it as the first of nice weather after a chilly winter. The birds are singing, the leaves are starting to sprout on the trees, the water on the creek looks crystal clear. In fact, I can think of no better time then this to get baptized, (the water is a bit cold). Looking down at the water, I now can visualize a preacher in a white robe leading someone out in the shallow water to be immersed.

4. The Temptation of Jesus Keyword: Hare (R)

In the garden of Eden, Satan was a snake, Jesus I see as being white as snow. In the temptation of Jesus, Satan tries to devour Jesus. I made a simple visual of a snake eating a pure white rabbit, half of the hare in it's mouth.

5. The Fulfillment of the Law Keyword: Wall (L)

The fulfillment of the law is like the Ten Commandments. It lists a few of the commandments. So I associate God's great hand coming out of heaven with a pointing finger, and with this finger he engraves the laws in the wall.

6. Prayer and Fasting Keyword: Shoe (SH)

I want you to pay especial attention to this association because as you go to other books of the Bible, you will notice the similar subject use for this example. Fasting is to do without food. When I fast, after a few days I feel so hungry that I think that I could eat my shoe. Visualize a shoe with the big toe sticking out where someone took a bite out of it.

7. Judging Others Keyword: Key (K)

Here I see the judge up behind his big fancy desk, looking down upon the person who committed the crime that caused him to be judged in the first place. It is the poor convicts unlucky day. The judge locked him up and threw away the key.

8. The Healings Keyword: Wave (V)
The Preacher waved his hands over the sick woman while he prayed and the woman was healed.

9. The Galling of Matthew Keyword: Pa (P)
When little Matthew was sitting in class, he heard his name called over the P.A. system to come to the office. His father was calling Matthew.

10. Sending Out the Twelve Disciples Keyword: Dice (TS)
The largest number you can roll on a pair of dice is 12.

11. Jesus and John the Baptist Keyword: Toad (TT)
My description of a toad is not only a amphibian or frog, but I also take a slang use of the word which is someone who might be a tattle tale or a messenger. In this example I am going to use the slang portion. I visualize this "toad" running between Jesus and John the Baptist giving each one a message from the other.

12. Lord of the Sabbath Keyword: Tin (TN)
Think of Jesus walking through a garden picking grains of wheat and placing them in a tin pie pan, and he is doing this on the Sabbath, the day of rest! It is allowable because he is the Lord of the Sabbath.

13. The Parables Keyword: Tomb (TM)
It is a dark night, the moon is full. Kids gather at the cemetery to tell each other scary stories. Telling stories is another way of saying: telling parables.

14. John the Baptist Beheaded Keyword: Tar (TR)
This one was a little hard for me because I did not want to sound disrespectful, but for the purpose of memory, I have to use some things that just are not politically correct. So for this visualization I see a person in a guillotine and there is a used tar bucket set under them to catch the head.

15. Clean and Unclean Keyword: Tail (TL)

Imagine the long tail of a cow and think of a short curly tail of the pig. The cow represents the clean, and the pig represents the unclean.

16. Jesus Predicts His Death Keyword: Tissue (TSh)
If Jesus was to come to me and tell me that he will be dying on the cross in the near future, I would need a tissue to wipe away the tears.

17. The Transfiguration Keyword: Tack (TK)
I am a very nice person but if you put a tack on my seat and I sit on it, I will transform into something ugly.

18. Greatest in the Kingdom of Heaven Keyword: Taffy (TV)
As we all know, children are the greatest in the kingdom of heaven, so I imagine seeing angels in the form of little children. I associate my thinking to seeing a little angel eating taffy, wearing pajamas with a #1 printed on the front.

19. Divorce Keyword: Tub (TP)
Imagine a scroll being a divorce decree and it is floating in a tub filled with water. This is when you know your marriage is washed up.

20. Two Blind Men Receive Sight Keyword: Nose (NS)
Two Jewish friends who have been blind since birth have just been healed. Holding each other by the shoulders they slowly open their eyes and the first thing they see is their friends big nose.

21. Jesus at the Temple Keyword: Net (NT)
Jesus walks into the temple and there is all kinds of people selling their wears. It looks like a big flea market and dividing each sellers area is a mosquito net. Jesus tears down the nets and tells the retailers to get out of the temple.

22. Whose Son is Christ? Keyword: Nanny (NN)
A nanny is taking care of a child and the kid is driving the nanny insane. She asks the child: "Who are you the son of?"

23. The Seven Woes Keyword: Name (NM)
Jesus said "Woe to you, you vipers, you hypocrites." Can you name the seven woes?

24. Signs of the End of the Age Keyword: Near (NR)

Some keywords fit almost as if they were written especially for what we are trying to remember. A man is holding a sign that reads: The End is Near.

25. The Parable of the Talents Keyword: Nail (NL)

A talent in the Bible was a large sum of money equal to about two years wages. Today coins are used and they are round but in my visual, I see sticks of gold being carried and they look like golden nails.

26. The Lord's Supper Keyword: Wench (NSH)

All you respected and wonderful women out there, do not send hate mail. This is strictly used for memory science only. As the Men were sitting around the supper table, who do you think served them? The wench!

27. The Crucifixion Keyword: Ink (NK)

As Christ Jesus our Lord and savior was crucified on the cross. A sign was placed above his head. Written in ink was: King of the Jews.

28. The Resurrection Keyword: Navy (NV)

When a boat sinks in the water, the Navy fills it full of air and raises it to the surface. Jesus was raised from the dead.

The Gospel of Matthew
Review

There are 28 chapters in the Gospel of Matthew. Write down the outline for all 28 chapters. Do not look back to check your answers until you fill in all 28 chapter subjects. Just skip over the one that you can not recall. After you complete the outline, go back and check your answers by comparing them to the original outline. For those chapters that you could not remember. Go back and review the Story Telling System or even create your own story.

Pill in the blanks of the outline for the Gospel of Matthew:

10.	19.
11.	20.
12.	21.

13.   22.

14.   23.

15.   24.

16.   25.

17.   26.

18.   27.

                                 28.

Write what chapter answers the question:

Jesus being tempted by Satan? _____
What chapter was the blind guys healed? _____
Who is the greatest in heaven? _____
The Lord's Supper? _____
Matthew is being called? _____
We should not judge others? _____
Can I get a divorce? _____
Jesus predicts his death? _____
The story of the birth of Christ? _____
Signs of the end of ages? _____
Jesus transformed into light? _____
John sent a message to Jesus? _____
Where do I find the law I should follow? _____

To check your answers. Go back to the original outline and compare your answers. If you missed any, review the story telling section and rewrite the outline once again.

CHAPTER NINE
THE GOSPEL OF MARK

(subtitle: A Friend)

The Outline of Mark

The Story Telling System

The Review of Mark

The Gospel of Mark

Chapter #

The calling of the first disciples
Jesus questioned about fasting
The appointing of the 12 apostles
Jesus calms the storm
The healing of the demon-possessed man
Jesus feeds the five thousand
The faith of a mother
Peter's confession of Christ
Whoever is not against us is for us
The rich man
The withered fig tree
Paying taxes to Caesar
The day and hour unknown
Jesus arrested
Jesus before Pilate
The resurrection

The Book of Mark (A Friend) Story Telling System

1. Galling of the first disciples Keyword: Tea (T)
Here I visualize my friend and I are sitting around drinking tea, looking through our yearbook, and calling all of our old friends,

2. Jesus questioned about fasting Keyword: Noah (N)
My friend and I are hanging out with Jesus and my friend ask's Jesus, "Did Noah have to fast since he only took two of each animal onto the ark?"

3. The appointing of the 12 apostles Keyword: Me (M)
Me and my friend are appointed to be two of the twelve apostles in the church play.

4. Jesus calms the storm Keyword: Hare (R)
My friend comes over and his hair is wildly messed up. I ask him what happened and he said that there is a big storm outside. Maybe we should wait for it to calm before going out.

5. The demon-possessed man Keyword: Wall (L)

My friend has a wall that surrounds his house. There is a crazy man that hangs out at the corner of the wall. He acts as if he is demon-possessed.

6. Jesus feeds the five thousand Keyword: Shoe (SH)

Imagine five thousand people walking over to your house. They are all hungry. They see that you and your friend ordered pizza. They all want some so they rush over you and your friend. You are trampled. All you see is the shoes of the five thousand hungry people as they step past you and your friend.

7. The faith of a mother Keyword: Key (K)

My friend owns a very nice house and he wanted someone to give a spare key to, just in case he lost his. He gave the spare key to his mother because he has faith in his mother.

8. Peter's confession of Christ Keyword: Wave (V)

My friend and Peter were out late one night. They got arrested. The police asked Peter if he would like to confess to a crime. He waved his rights and confessed.

9. Whoever is not against us is for us Keyword: Pay (P)

Jesus paid the price for my friend's salvation. Now those who are not against my friend must be a Christian like him. They must be for him.

10. The rich man Keyword: Dice (DC)

My friend likes to play dice and he often win's. Now he is a rich man.

11. The withered fig tree Keyword: Toad (TD)

In my friends back yard, there is a big tree that is dying. And I noticed this toad that made it's home in the withered tree.

12. Paying taxes to Caesar Keyword: Tin (TN)

My friend keeps all his spare change in this tin box. There is enough money there that he might have to pay taxes on it.

13. The day and hour unknown Keyword: Tomb (TM)

My friend is going to die. He says that we all will die someday, we just don't know the hour or day.

14. Jesus arrested Keyword: Tar (TR)
My friend and I enjoy four wheeling. One day my friend drove around some barricades and drove over a freshly paved street. He left deep tire tracks in the tar. He was arrested.

15. Jesus before Pilate Keyword: Tail (TL)
My friend wanted to get married, so he hired a plane to fly a banner saying "marry me". The banner looked like a long tail behind the plane that the pilot was flying.

16. The resurrection Keyword: Tissue (TSh)
My friend needed a tissue when he heard that Jesus died. But threw the tissue up in the air in celebration, when he learned of the resurrection.

The book of Mark (a friend) Review

Write down the outline for all 16 chapters of Mark. Do not look back to check your answers until you completely fill in the outline. Just skip over the one that you can not recall. After you complete the outline, go back and review your answers by comparing them to the original outline. If you have problems with any particular chapter, go back and create your own story.
Fill in the blanks of the outline for the book of Mark:

6.	11.
7.	12.
8.	13.
9.	14.
10.	15.
	16.

Write what chapter answers the question:

Jesus arrested? _____
The rich man? _____

Jesus calms the storm? ____
The faith of a mother? ____
The withered fig tree? ____
The day and hour unknown? ____
Paying taxes to Caesar? ____
Jesus before Pilate? ____
The resurrection? ____
Healing of the demon-possessed man? ____
Appointing of the twelve apostles? ____
Who is not against us is for us? ____
Jesus feeds five thousand? ____
Calling of the first disciples? ____
Jesus questioned about fasting? ____

To check your answers. Go back to the original outline and compare your answers. If you miss any, review the story telling section and then rewrite the outline once again.

CHAPTER TEN
THE GOSPEL OF LUKE

(subtitle: Doctor)

The Outline of Luke

The Story Telling System

The Review of Luke

The Gospel of Luke
(SubTitie: Doctor)

Chapter#

The Birth of Jesus Foretold
Jesus Presented in the Temple
John the Baptist Prepares the Way
Jesus Rejected at Nazareth
The Man With Leprosy
Love for Enemies
Jesus Raises a Widow's Son
Lamp on a Stand
The Cost of Following Jesus
Jesus Sends Out the Seventy-two
Jesus and Beelzebub
Watchfulness
Repent or Perish
The Cost of Being a Disciple
The Parable of the Lost Son
The Rich Man and Lazarus
The Coming of the Kingdom of God
The Little Children and Jesus
The Triumphal Entry
Resurrection and Marriage
The Widow's Offering
Peter Disowns Jesus
Jesus' Burial
Jesus Appears to the Disciples

The Gospel of Luke (Doctor)
Story Telling System

1. The Birth of Jesus Foretold Keyword: Tea (T)

Our Doctor is an Obstetrician. And his "T" is the tools of his trade. The Doctors most important tool is his knowledge, he is able to look at a patient and foretell when the birth is due.

2. Jesus Presented in the Temple Keyword: Noah (N)

I view Noah as a deeply religious man, since God intrusted Noah with build-ing the ark, which saved Noah's family and gave mankind a new start. I can easily visualize Noah when his first child was born after the flood. Immediately after the Doctor delievered the baby to present the child in the Temple to the Lord. And this helps in remembering that Jesus was presented in the Temple.

3. John the Baptist Prepares the Way Keyword: May or Me (M)

Me and the Doctor. I was racing ahead of the Doctor preparing the way, so he could get to the Hospital quickly and deliever the baby.

4. Jesus Rejected at Nazareth Keyword: Hare or Hair (R)

Our Doctor is going bald, so he decided to try hair implants. He underwent the procedure only to be disappointed when his body rejected them. Now in your mind as you imagine the Doctors hair implants being rejected, just remember that Jesus was rejected also, but He was rejected at Nazareth.

5. The Man with Leprosy Keyword: Wall (L)

I visualize the Doctors wall being an area where patients with communicable diseases are kept. This is where the man with leprosy is kept, to prevent the spread of disease.

6. Love for Enemies Keyword: Shoe (SH)

The Doctor had his shoes stolen the other day, later when he was making rounds a man came into the Emergency room with a gun shot wound. The Doc-tor recognized him as the man who had stolen his shoes, but he still had to show love to his enemy and try to save his life.

7. Jesus Raises a Widow's Son Keyword: Key (K)

Our Doctors key is Jesus and knowing the Blessings he has recieved from the Lord. He decided to try and show the same type of love to the local community he serves. Knowing how many children were growing up without fathers. He started a program to help raise a widow's son, to help mold him and instruct him and to make Jesus the key to his life.

8. Lamp on a Stand Keyword: Wave (V)

The Doctor has a large yacht. And I visualize him out in the gulf with the waves tossing the yacht around so much that he has to secure the lamp on a stand to keep it from getting broke.

9. The Cost of Following Jesus Keyword: Pay (P)
The Doctor is a Christian, and when a believer comes in and has no money for medical care, he pays the cost for them since they follow Jesus.

10. Jesus Sends Out the Seventy-two Keyword: Dice (TS)
If you think back to Matthews dice, we visualized the largest number you can roll on a pair of dice is 12. And that was the sending out of the 12 Disciples. Now with that in mind imagine the Doctor is 72 years old and his dice is: Jesus sends out the 72.

11. Jesus and Beelzebub Keyword: Toad (TT)
The Doctor has a pet toad named Bub. And so he can keep track of Bub, he put a collar with bells on Bub (Beelzebub).

12. Watchfulness Keyword: Tin (TN)
I see the Doctor with a tin telescope looking up in the sky at the stars, he says: "I'm watching for Jesus."

13. Repent or Perish Keyword: Tomb (TM)
The Doctor has seen so many lives wasted through violence and drug use. So every chance he gets he preaches to the young people: "Repent or Perish." The Doctor does not want any to go to their tomb and be lost for Eternity.

14. The Cost of Being a Disciple Keyword: Tar (TR)
The Doctor believes that as a Christian he has a responsibility to help people, its part of the cost of being a Disciple of Christ. When a poor family needed a new tar roof, he was one of the first to volunteer to help replace the tar roof.

15. The Parable of the Lost Son Keyword: Tail or Tale (TL)
The Doctors tale is the story of his lost son. The boy who had everything but ran away from home. Born with a silver spoon in his mouth, all thing were possible and within his reach, but he squandered his wealth in wild living to a point of being homeless. But when he finally hit the bottom, it was through God's Grace and Mercy that he came back to his senses and returned to his father, who loved

him and restored him. Fortunately the tale of the Doctors lost son has a happy ending.

16. The Rich Man and Lazarus Keyword: Tissue (TSH)
The Doctors tissue represents the choice the Doctor and each one of us must make. Imagine Heaven and Hell separated by a tissue. On one side is the rich man in agony in the flames of Hell, on the other side of the tissue is Lazarus recieving all the good things he never had during his life. The Doctors tissue is the story of the rich man and Lazarus, the Doctor through faith made the right choice and accepted Jesus.

17. The Coming of the Kingdom of God Keyword: Tack (TK)
The Doctor has a postcard of the Kingdom of God tacked on his office door, and above it he wrote: "coming soon."

18. The Little Children and Jesus Keyword: Taffy (TV)
The Doctor always gives candy to the little children when they come to his office, because he loves them just like Jesus does.

19. The Triumphal Entry Keyword: Tub (TP)
The Doctor lives out in the country and for a hobby raises donkeys. When I was out at his place the other day I seen this donkey getting a drink out of the Doctors tub, and it made me think of when Jesus sent his disciple to get a donkey, so he could make his triumphal entry into Jerusalem. So the Doctors tub is the "Triumphal Entry."

20. Resurrection and Marriage Keyword: Nose (NS)
The Doctor married this girl with a big nose, and one of the first things she wanted after they were married was to find someone to reconstruct (resurrect) her nose.

21. The Widow's Offering Keyword: Net (NT)
The doctors fishing net was woven together by the widow as an offering for all of his services.

22. Peter Disowns Jesus Keyword: Nanny (NN)
The doctors nanny is faithful and would never disown him or his son Peter.

23. Jesus' Burial Keyword: Name (NM)

The doctors name will appear in the book of life since he has lived his life for the Lord. He knows when he dies and is buried, it will be just like Jesus' burial. He will be with God for eternity.

24. Jesus Appears to the Disciples Keyword: Near (NR)

The doctor, as a Christian, believes the end is near and is waiting for Jesus to appear to his disciples.

The Gospel of Luke (Doctor)
Review

There are 24 chapters in the Gospel of Luke. Write down the outline for all 24 chapters. Do not look back to check your answers until you fill in all 24 chapter subjects. Just skip over the one that you can not recall. After you complete the outline, go back and check your answers by comparing them to the original outline. For those chapters that you could not remember. Go back and review the Story Telling System or even create your own story.

Fill in the blanks of the outline for the Gospel of Luke:

9.   17.

10.   18.

11.   19.

12.   20.

13.   21.

14.   22.

15.   23.

16.   24.

Write what chapter answers the question:

Love for enemies? _____
The rich man and Lazarus? _____
The triumphal entry? _____
The cost of following Jesus? _____
Repent or perish? _____

The birth of Jesus foretold? _____
Peter disowns Jesus? _____
John the baptist prepares the way? _____
Jesus and Beelzebub? _____
The coming of the Kingdom of God? _____
Lamp on a stand? _____
The man with leprosy? _____
Jesus appears to the disciples? _____
Jesus presented in the temple? _____
The widows offering? _____
Watchfulness? _____
The parable of the lost son? _____
The little children and Jesus? _____

To check your answers. Go back to the original outline and compare your answers. If you missed any, review the story telling section and rewrite the outline once again.

CHAPTER ELEVEN
THE GOSPEL OF JOHN

(subtitle: Dad's Name)

The Outline of John

The Story Telling System

The Review of Matthew

The Gospel of John

Chapter #

  The Word becomes flesh
  Jesus changes water into wine
  Jesus teaches Nicodemus
  Jesus talks to the Samaritan woman
  The healing pool
  Jesus the bread of life
  Is Jesus the Christ?
  The validity of Jesus testimony
  Jesus heals a man born blind
 The shepherd and his flock
 The death of Lazarus
 Jesus anointed at Bethany
 Jesus predicts His betrayal
 Jesus promises the Holy Spirit
 The vine and the branches
 The works of the Holy Spirit
 Jesus prays
 The high priest questions Jesus
 The death of Jesus
 The empty tomb
 Jesus catch of fish

The Gospel of John (Dad's name) Story Telling System

1. The Word became flesh Keyword: Tea (T)

Your father's "T" is the New Testament. He explains to you that the Word of God became flesh when Jesus was born. You can visualize your father studying the Bible. Next to him is a glass of tea. You might think that he is eating the Word and drinking the Tea.

2. Jesus changes water into wine Keyword: Noah (N)

If it rained and flooded for 40 days and 40 nights, and our dad was stuck on a boat full of animals. I think he would want all that rain water to be wine.

3. Jesus teaches Nicodemus Keyword: Me (M)

My dad and I smoked for many years. We decided to quit the habit together. So we bought the nicotine patch. "Nicodemus CQ".

4. Jesus talks to the Samaritan women Keyword: Hare (R)

When my dad knew he was going to meet the pretty Samaritan woman, he felt the need to comb his hair to look good.

5. The healing at the pool Keyword: Wall (L)

My dad put in a heated pool in the back yard. The hot water gave a healing effect. He had to put up a wall around the pool to keep the neighbors out.

6. Jesus the bread of life Keyword: Shoe (Sh)

My dad liked to bake. He would often attempt to make bear claws. But they would look more like a shoe then a bears foot. The donut was often as tough to eat as a leather shoe, but when your really hungry and there is nothing else to eat. It becomes the bread of life.

7. Is Jesus the Christ? Keyword: Key (K)

Do you remember the craze with WWJD? WWJD meant: What would Jesus do? You could find them on many key chains, bracelets, and necklaces. Instead of a key chain with WWJD, we are going to give our dad a key chain that asks: Is Jesus the Christ?

8. The validity of Jesus testimony Keyword: Wave (V)

When ever my dad waves, he gives us the v sign meaning peace. We call it the wave-v which is the validity or proof that he was in the peace and love era.

9. Jesus heals a man born blind Keyword: Pay (P)

My dad would go to the carnival and pay money to see what they called a miracle. But all he had to do is read in the Bible how jesus healed the blind. He wouldn't have to pay for that.

10. The shepherd and flock Keyword: Dice (DC)

My dad rolled the dice by having so many kids. Now he has a flock that he has to shepherd. It is a gamble to have so many kids.

11. The death of Lazarus Keyword: Toad (TD)

I visualize a dead toad in my dads driveway. When I yell at my dad for driving over the toad, he says that it is not dead, it is only sleeping. When I go check, the toad is hopping away.

12. Jesus anointed at Bethany Keyword: Tin (TN)
My father has a fancy tin pitcher. He says it is for anointing people with oil. I think it looks more like a tin pitcher used to serve water with. He said that when Jesus was in Bethany, He was anointed with oil and the oil was kept in small tin's just like it.

13. Jesus predicts His betrayal Keyword: Tomb (TM)
When my dad past away, all the kids felt betrayed because he didn't put any of us in his will. Now none of them will even visit his tomb.

14. Jesus promises the Holy Spirit Keyword: Tar (TR)
I easily associate tar to oil. So when my dad anointed me with the tar or oil, he promised me that I would receive the Holy Spirit.

15. The vine and the branches Keyword: Tail (TL)
The curly branches on the grape vine reminds me of the tail of a pig. My dad always told us that he is the branch and the kids are the vines, and if we do not act accordingly, he can cut us off.

16. The works of the Holy Spirit Keyword: Tissue (TSh)
Remember when you were in grade school and you use to make ghosts out of two tissues? One was balled up, another draped over it and tied in the middle? Now imagine that you have to dust your room with that tissue ghost. This would be work of the ghost. I might also use the visual of the Holy Spirit inside me holding a tissue to clean up the mess in my life.

17. Jesus prays Keyword: Tack (TK)
I have a little postcard that has the words that Jesus prayed on it. I tack it to my wall to remind me of how Jesus would pray.

18. The high priest question Jesus Keyword: Taffy (TV)
When I was younger, my dad would always question me on where I got the candy I would eat. Now I know how Jesus might have felt.

19. The death of Jesus Keyword: Tub (TB)

This is a terrible memory story but it makes it's point. I visualize my dads tub filled with blood and the cross hanging over the tub, on the wall.

20. The empty tomb Keyword: Nose (NS)

I can see my dad rubbing his nose at the tomb of Jesus and saying that the tomb must be empty because he doesn't smell death. Or if your dad has a big nose like mine. You might just think that his nose looks like a big empty tomb.

21. Jesus catch of fish Keyword: Net (NT)

My dad loves to fish, so I can see him throwing out a net and catching fish.

The Book of John (Dads name) Review

There are 21 chapters in the book of John. Write down the outline for all 21 chapters. Do not look back to check your answers until you fill in all 21 chapter subjects. Just skip over the one that you can not recall. After you complete the outline, go back and check your answers by comparing them to the original outline. For those chapters that you could not remember. Go back and review the Story Telling system or even create your own story.

Fill in the blanks of the outline for the book of John:

8.	15.
9.	16.
10.	17.
11.	18.
12.	19.
13.	20.
14.	21.

Write what chapter answers the question:

The empty tomb? _____
Jesus Prays? _____
Jesus arrested? _____

The healing pool? ____
The Word becomes flesh? ____
Is Jesus the Christ? ____
Jesus catches the fishes? ____
The death of Lazarus? ____
Jesus anointed in Bethany? ____
The promise of the Holy Spirit? ____
The work of the Holy Spirit? ____
The shepherd and the flock? ____
The vine and the branches? ____
Jesus heals the blind man? ____
The validity of Jesus testimony? ____

   To check your answers. Go back to the original outline and compare your answers. If you missed any, review the story telling section and rewrite the outline once again.

About the Author

Through the study of mnemonics, Twitty improved his memory capacity by using intense visualization, memory association and finally initiated the Infinity technique that changed his life by opening the doors to a photographic memory. Now Twitty teaches memory as a ministry improving the lives of others, spiritually, professionally, and socially.

978-0-595-37506-6
0-595-37506-5

www.ingramcontent.com/pod-product-compliance
Lightning Source LLC
Chambersburg PA
CBHW030413290526
45785CB00004B/1982

* 9 7 8 0 5 9 5 3 7 5 0 6 6 *